Caroline

Poetry by
Jonah Gabriel

without company 2007

Thin Line 2009

yesterdaysmile press

Jonah Gabriel

Caroline

selected poems

Copyright © 2013 by Jonah Gabriel. All rights reserved.

yesterdaysmile press 2013 (ISBN: 978-0-615-78739-8)

No part of this book may be reproduced or transmitted in any form or by any means without written permission by the author.

Cover design by Betty Schulte
Author photo by Drew Snider
Edited by Vada Bodimer and Ivy Walsh

Type is Times New Roman

Printed in the United States of America

IN MEMORIAM

Jordan Denae Snider

1992 – 2011

Contents

breathing tube	10
white	11
funeral	14
with silence	15
the Priest	16
butterfly	17
the box	19
dirty	21
untitled	22
breath	23
halo	24
Oaklawn	26
crack in the sidewalk	28
seductive	29
the dying child	30
counterproductive remission	31
Red door	32
mexico	34
machines	35
silhouette	37
love	38
slow	39
spitting off the balcony	40
in red	41
eighteen	42
Mercy	43
atrophy	44
illusionary	45
saturday Love	47
dance	49
glass	50
letter	52
letter remix	53
Charlie on the move	54
Accumulated Occupancy	56
Windsor south	57
black and white	58
vicious	59
alkaline	60
alchemy	62
reunion	63
life	65

Contents Continued

reaper man	67
crimson	68
heartbeat	69
paper eyes	71
2 into 1	72
tonic	73
conjoined	75
for ced cohesion	76
sibling	77
fracture	79
Caroline	84
Untitled	86

Caroline

breathing tube

resuscitation… squeeze air in
hold…
compressions…
hands to chest
push
one, one thousand
two, two one thousand
three
squeeze air in

crisis

conscious sedation
painless
blinking eyes
tears form
opened ears
code blue
crashing

37 minutes

the phone rings
waking dreamy
eight 30 sadness

decompression

and the bed stirred silent
two by one hand to hands
keeping the body warm
as the nurse and the required
Jesus representative
stood idle arms crossed
the room was full
all but the soul

in peace
as the breathing tube was removed
beginning
a four hour goodbye
lasting

white

the dust
all around, the dust
exploding in, breathing in, exhaling out

eyes focus
blurry focus, eyes
sunshine bright, turning red

in the shadows, the morning shadows
mourning
black rein, black suit, black painted eyes
April

pause…break…pause

once while under the stars gazing
-the moon was full-
fall break, winter's cold flurry, fury
two alone in Falls Park
lips pressed into lips
and the two became one for a moment
hearts joined, hands and arms tangled
a crossword of bodies creating a life
full of hope, the audacity of love
she spoke

the background noise
white
speaks in tongues
uninterrupted

never.   coming.   home.

mirror mirror
masked to hide emotions bare
torn into flesh
primal

left unspoken
all the lessons from a father to his daughter
full of pride
a lifetime of "I love you"
now quietly said in private

time stops

my mind restarts…

from the phone call
saying get to the hospital
that woke a slumbering body
to the black Saturn screaming three digits
with the rain misting
and the squeaking of Nikes on waxed tile
as these feet ran confused down the corridor
to your mother with reddened eyes
slowly explaining
the grey concrete wall so cold
as the back pressed against trying to steady
weakening knees
head collapsing into hands disbelieving
the slow walk into the blue room
where you laid so peacefully
breathing tube still in place
the covers were pulled up to your chin
just like when I used to tuck you in
I reached out my hand
and took yours
I stroked your hair and rubbed the crown of your nose
phone calls made to family in-between uncontrolled emotion

your hand turning cold, no matter how much I rubbed it
I just sat there, next to you, helpless

four hours I stayed praying to a God that I couldn't find reason to believe in

time stopped

and my mind restarts

funeral

all at once the rains came
Friday morning seizing
as the blooming April flowers
catapult emotions in plain sight

black suit pressing

hand to skin cold resemblance
245 standing still
in an empty room
two people once but never again
touching

a single heart struggling
while the background fills
pictures flash in and out music
whispering note to note
eyes closed

empty and hollow

the preacher man with his God speech
mentions vessels and how the body meant nothing
that death was the natural process and that Gods plan
was being followed
all the while the baby boy with his blue eyes penetrating
focused on everything but the ending
as the first child's soul ascends

from the back to the front one last visit
silent thoughts filled with love praying for hope
even then the tears spoke louder than words
and in the midst a stranger's embrace steadied
unbalanced knees when the heart stopped beating

730 hands to rail looking at curled hair that was never curly
the mind raced as it realized that this was the last time
for a father to see his daughter
and as the quiet filled the room
the last goodbye continues

with silence
in

the bottle stands statue
empty
a testament of wishes

the four ounce tumbler
gripped
sweating in a shaky hand

the ice cubes
melting
along with the last bit of courage

black and white is never

with silence the words start forming
in silence mouth to ear
being

a smoky room swells
alcoholic breath
scream

the last exhale swirl
snake eye focused
regret

uncovered in denial

cold hands touch
wrapping shoulder to shoulder
alone

and the echo follows
movement stationary
gone

in pale light
the sun rises coloring
vanilla skies

always is never

the Priest

the day to day, scabbed knees, the day to day,
on the outside, filter ash, falling from the end.
screaming, to, the deafness, passing away, against
stone walls, the migraine traces, covered, in focus
catching shadows faltering, in the watchful eyes,
without arms sheltering denial, hands around the neck,
strangled, in words, in praise, the day to day, the day
by day, crucifix

the digression of reality, takes the strangest road to mentality

butterfly *(the burial)*

under the half alive half dead oak tree, leaves
green and branches bare, resting

marble and bronze

and they waited for the mother
to read your words

and they waited in their orange Case backhoe
for Blue October to be silenced

and they waited in their white GMC
for Grandpa Dan to quote Mother Teresa

baby boy blue was fidgeting next to a father
begging as the wind tussled the freshly mowed grass
and the leaves rustled in the background where
the four leaf clovers dwell

and they waited in their golf cart with the Oaklawn
logo proudly shown

and they waited
for the permanent tomb to be filled with Zerbert, and rose petals,
rocks from the coast, and you, as the father held you for the last
time

and they waited in the long hot summer sun
even as a butterfly flew into view and rested next to you
almost keeping you company for eternity as the tomb was
slowly being sealed

and they waited for an hour and a half
even as the last tear fell and the father walked away
wishing for more time

the wind slowed as the tent and chairs were removed
the ground shook time stood still
as you, the precious daughter, were buried

and with thumbs tied / arms crossed
fingers form the wings

butterfly

the box

this isn't tragic
just a cold inhumane human act
lead by Jesus and his
goddamn fucked up sense of life…

taken too soon

eighteen

human touch
in dreams rapid eyes
wake the stirring
wake a restless soul

the door is open
letting in the rain
in cold a faltering heart
sits in a plastic chair
ever watching never
and it came to pass
Saturday

hand to hand

in haste
rage
hate
consequence
taking place
full of damage
remorse

as the voices crowd
asking what is next
moving forward
words heal
words trap
words lead
"look how beautiful destruction is"

time slows with whiskey and wine
another cigarette flips
the smoke lingers

like the eyeliner that captured
hazel eyes peaceful

sealed in the box
buried under the bronze plaque
in waiting

it becomes so much to bear
protecting knowing the protection failed

with condolences
then comes the memory that Friday
laughter and smiles were profoundly radiating
and maybe the happiness
that was always just out of reach
was finally in grasp

but that is only hope
because all that is left
are the pages upon pages of thoughts
truth denial realization
that death was the only true way
to achieve happiness

6teen days
still in the plastic chair
ever waiting
the answers will never come
the truth although known
will never be admitted to
and the heart weeps
as the fingers rub the star
containing the beginning the middle
the end

dirty

dirty tempo
slum to slum she speaks
of miracles and praise
Jesus walking
breath to thought
hand in
soul tearing
corner eyes saline
belief of plausible
dancing in flame
she speaks
with the cloak around her throat
choking

untitled

faux suede cling
like tiny fingers
massaging
B.o.B. is screaming
NyNy revolutions
as Jesus lays
on a rusted chain
strangling

purple around the wrist
an 18 year old
fashion statement
turned into
an 18 year old
memorial
lasting

in motion
never in, motion
stability
lack there of
distance
distant in
destruction

the last
of physical memory
withers through
clouded
visions
of perception in
reality

breath

with triggers in, mainlined
Jesus falling from the,
cross out the name, creeping

in flame, inhale, calming
darkness echoes, light
consuming, with shadows

palpations weaken, exhale
another line, the clock ticks
away, with eyes closed

to the beat, heart
pumping regret, traveling
from vein to, release

inhale…exhale…inhale…exhale…

halo

foggy midnight transcontinental

beautiful ligaments retinal

under pass a moon full
angels come in masked
naked in oblivion
out of control

whispers in silence
strangling

tempered
in cold resonance
a whiskey bottle stands alone
empty

withholding promises
the ice melts slow
as dreams mix
with obscurity and delusional activities

scissor feathers steal

amputated in corners shadowed

in a dirty white stained robe
beneath a threshold holding
abandoned child weeping
in lambs blood

the night wanes
a broken halo flaunt
corrosive miracle blend
sin and fortitude on knees

blaspheme hands clasp

flooded vision deafened

looking up with tears lining
a darkening suicidal religion
forcing a stuttering heart
to plead with its last beat

breathless passionate lips
closing in with every verse
rip through pages upon
for last rights saving

Oaklawn

there is…
as the heart lets go,
nothing, but loss…

one hundred and eighty days of temporary

and she speaks to everyone but…

the nightmares' terror has become,
struggling to catch breathing,
lacking, as midnight infomercials
cast shadows in peripheral vision
sighting lines and shapes, "colours"

tomorrows promise, a memory,
while distance isn't the worry, silence
transforms the contradictory ambiance
that once spilled with-in moving lips now
tightly closed in cold, chapped…without

in pacing, hands wrap around
weathered hands
the grave covered in leaves
gold letters blending

on soiled knee's pleading, the wind picks
it's place to alter belief, but it is only
passing, as knee's still
bend on ground and hands lay
cold on bronze

away~
in regret
a numbing arm and closing vision
vessel toxic emissions,

stumbling through one day to the next
the facade has become more, the smile
is fake, the laughter is an actor
hitting his lines, as darkness slowly
closes around,
closes down

Autumn falls like salt into an opened wound
as breathing shutters, "remain calm"
clutching a star around the neck, the soundtrack
of life has become muted, while the world keeps spinning,
nothing has meaning, no future only endings,
only yesterday's smile still beaming…

crack in the sidewalk

haunted frames plastered in black hysteria pacing into the past racing away from the responsible lack of closure chewing on paper trails written in lies a scream a kick closer- the habit; and the noise white up the nose shrill in volume addict the secret in the attic warms with the sun in shivers the fallout has begun under stress and without clothes naked in the street the mask wearing thin as the ugly scars mend faster now that the closet is full and pain is lost in the tourniquet lying in the motion of understanding / regarding apathy passively given as advancing sleep deprivation visions 3 am pizza microwaved on ten percent forever cast a shadow as 837 closes down the rain streaks the wipers running 90 in a 45 time stands in the hourglass filling with sand traumatizing the wingless demon residing deep inside the chills choke in the midst of spring unread emails and text remain as the dial only focuses on a unchanged voicemail where the voice is calling holding attention the 14 seconds of yesterday living in denial in denial with two angels holding back hair out of eyes misery thrives tears climb in desperation lacking gravity crazy unwinds and lies on the couch making itself at home pulling the covers tight around the neck losing the will to breathe tomorrow cannot come too soon
reuniting

seductive

seductive tempo
body to body she speaks
of heaven and light
Jesus taking
sin for sin
cleansing
soul bending
sticks and stones
closing down
collapsing around
she speaks
with her crucifix straining
dirty knees

the dying child

darkness calls out
full of stars and moons
closet
weeping slight
tears run backwards
memory hands

rusted motion
in

wrapped cloth
baby pink
shelter

stainless steel
the virgin falls

linoleum stained

8 am
middle afternoon
fluorescent eyes

migraine in space
the door closes
keeping

remedy
bright brown fade
suffocating

cigarette smoldering ashtray over

linoleum stained

counterproductive remission

through the dust
whipping post engaged;
self-serving plausibility

the ticket is one way
coastal coach
Siberian rain forest ch-
-oke

a blacked out star light
creeping up
stretched out arms
fly

transgression sits on the pull out tray
paper mug filling
courage to scream\release

no smoking in baggage

turbulent south
shifting winds
seatbelt applied

liquid transfer
fail to grasp

denial

Red Door

leave it to the mother fuckers
the square ass have no life
drinking beer on a Monday morning
mother fuckers to start shit

as if they know, know breath and escape
the hyperventilate, closet paranoia of the darkness
closing in, the shrinking atmosphere of hope
as if they know, know of funerals and loss
of pain and regret of missing and want
as if they know, know, while they run their
foul mouths talking shit about moving on
letting go, acceptance
as if they know…

there is tranquility in blood, life
seeping onto the sheets from the sharpened
razorblade made of German Steel, there is
the sweet lack of vision in fluttering eyes and the
heat around the cut, cut through, deep into bone,
penetrating, body refusing

onto the floor, the puddle grows ever deeper
with every breath the escape, the hurt
the tears, the violence of hate, time is…

and with blacked out eyes and a clowns grin,
wicked, it begins

and lost cannot explain, barely understanding
the undeserved comprehension of drowning
in apprehension, in complication, the ward
binds wrist and feet, mind slowly speaks, as scars
beg to rip away the feathered stitches and reopen,
let the work continue down, into the drain, in Earth
we have become, in ash we remain

fluorescent flicker, a mind numbing hum tearing
into confiscated drums, as the morning pudding served
with plastic spoons mixed with anti-anxiety and altered
clarity, it is in this state, state of state, the dreams begin
wide awake, eyes rotate and September evenings
with stars burning on a string, become something
enchanting

the three day memorial a six month
continual, required pills, forced breath,
stuttered heartbeat, the wake…
in black suit and purple tie adorning
the shoes have no buffer skin to soul
soul to ground the weight of the box
confounds, as hands to hands shaky
recall the memory of a baby girl first born
in the pink blanket, it contorts the moment
of the final resting

in bronze the cold November wind
shapes the bare landscape kneeling as
winter is approaching and snow will cover
the name 6 days out of seven

forever is…

mexico

fever fills shaking dreams
black and moving
crumble, walls seamless reactions
a ceiling fan's typhoon contradicting

in sweats, sweat rolls
across the cheeks through pouting lips
craving for the slightest hint
just breathe, a wondering mind states

the left hand tumbles from the bed and hangs
like a ghost, during, without
a shiver, feel, reaching, back, into
time stood still and yesterday smiled
as the clouds reached through and brought the darkness
into a unsteady heart

and the mirror spoke, as the third world power supply
wavered in and out, the mirror spoke of funerals,
death beds, of the graveyards need for coffins full,
of promises taken, and yet undelivered

intersecting broken triangles rapid eyes find favor
as the shadows slowly pull the sheets tighter to the throat
pausing as mumbled words choke in motives desperate

and as the lids close even tighter a tear makes it way finding
momentum while the right hand lands on the chest with a full fist
and force beating the heart back into submission even as the razor
blade dream pulses blood out of the left hand dangling

Jesus torture as the memory of cold skin to skin layer
unbridled in withered bandages cryptically holding
the beaten and scarred body

the silent scream, hoarse in a soured voice
struggling with a star around the neck
never letting the daughter go

open eyes

love is

machines

the beauty in contrast

crimson on white
the droplets spreading
from the external wound
from scars repeating
even the black carpet
is a glow, in life, the after flow
welcome to the show

and while thin it may be

it still sparkles in light
the face to face, memory
as steam clouds the vision
pain is tattooed into the brain
a constant reminder that nothing
comforting ever stays
comforting

the silence of machines

a future of screams with test tubes and medication
streaming live, as childproof caps no longer
as the daughter has passed and rest
six feet under

but joining has such a special ring

a pull of the strings, as the heart
monitor weeps, a cure maybe, but
in disguise the fight, would only be
to show the boy to hold dear
and that a fathers' love is everlasting

but the dream of heaven

although impeached sounds so ever inviting,
a father with his daughter laughing,
the struggle it seems is the choice between
a memory and life, hope or death, closing in or opening up
it is in this shelter of knowing
that this heart is forever divided
no matter the constant image that plays on reddened eyes

silhouette

the background noise
is where i find you
when the dark closes in
and i fall again
when everything crowds
and everyone crashes down
it is in that shadow that i
find solace and you
always

love

there is blood on the floor
dried droplets of purity
combined with saline shed
against terror filled dreams
ever watching the depths
of scars opening… just love

in the backroom darkened
the backroom where secrets hide
closets treasure the paper heart
pleading for understanding in
white October skies storming

rug burned knees bend
on contrast bare walls
guide eyes to the plastic cross
and the halo of thorns accepting
but as Jesus speaks the razorblade
corrupts and hollow becomes the name
saving… just love

middle afternoon visitation
as ash forms at the end of a Camel
under the oak tree the leaves
begin the blending, from Earth
we became, and in grave we
remain side by side a father
speaking from the first breath to the last…
just love

slow

slow tempo
air to air scream she speaks
of righteousness and the word
Jesus healing
touch to heart
heart to beat
breaking
soul ascending
covered in six feet
earth shaking
she speaks
with her angel wings
fluttering

spitting off the balcony

High frequency words scroll across migraine induced eyes becoming alone in the dark love sick and vomiting remorseful apologies continuing in spite of plastic hearts cracking in midnights moon sheltering. Razor blade tears falling, the sky forms dreams in colors running in spirit, faith in plans, this pill ends regret, as the gun shines in the metal tub splattered with dead skin cells and shampoo. The five bright globe lights induce shadows movement across the wall painted Alaskan white in memory we all fall once in a while, sweat spills into redness clotting perfect thought. Meanwhile the mirror dances to fluttering, blinking, as blackout approaches the knees shiver underweight shouldered, in doubt, still the nest on fiery tongues meant to endure love so it's told in carvings across the soul, hiding the truth in depths below. Losing feeling, the hands numb scribe the last words, apologies in rhythm, as chords of melody fill ears long ago deaf but cleansing. In hollow sharing the last smoke with a long forgotten ghost tattooed into depths so pure, breaking bad never felt so good with the body giving in, the ultimate sin. Beginning with the last swallow and a wish tasting revenge as the black mascara and eye liner run and hide into the tomb, mothers' womb, time drops to its knees forgiveness means closing the door, and walking away into nothing.

in red

violence / follow sheep
into black wonderment
purging storm clouds
razor blade teeth

Jesus speak
a twin with satanic divinity
the rain is flooding
bleeding in red

soul to soul one unto one
alcoholic slurring miss you kid
scars shaping stars
between cold and dust

fever pitched / secondary hesitation
breathless regret
in the dark life begins
condolences~

eighteen

infinite

crisis in dreams waking, heart seized,
a struggle to catch breathing, partial blindness
freezing, pulling into corners, watching

altered personality, cracking, Jesus and his fucking halo
waiting…

eight 30 tragic mourning, in cold, boxed
questioning sanity, plastic smiles haunting

a confusion running, seconds becoming
ink from veins stain, tomorrow wane

waiting for the end, and the confrontation: Jesus
and his Goddamn halo flaunting, dressed in black,
purple skin blending cuts into release, mentality
(a ward of possibilities)

Ambulance sirens screaming / blessed in red
3 miles from the graveyard pleading
collapsing, heart shaped monitors flat lining.

in mourning, dark eyes distant
numbness in touch, out of,
tears fall continuance, staggering, balance

the last days. cleansing, with shower steam
enveloping, as the rain swept clouds hesitate,
lightening crashes, releasing

Mercy

the background noise full
of strings and synthesizers over-
powering the softening voices to
a murmur, she lies dressed in purple
and black embroidered, surrounded by lace,
full of grace, the coffin brown, rented

the cloak spoke in tones tranquil, terrifying
tears down the face drowning

the dark filling, no stars, just grief

November winds set the mood-toxic
as prescriptions upon prescriptions fill
the cabinet to alleviate, to slow, to adjust
the calling razor blade stained in yesterdays
dirty blood, the shower steams fragile, as forced
scrubbing takes away a smile that faded before
the April rains came, and as night finally turned
dark, no stars, just pain remaining

secluded rehab as needles proceed the following
day with procedures meant to right the brain and slow
the self-induced bleed, dark eyes roll hazel and brown
as the showdown pulls the room into white

can You hear?
as tears fall on her grave
can You feel?
as this cross is ripped off the neck
can You see?
all the pain and grief overpowering
can You understand?
how much hatred and disbelief there is for You

atrophy

through the pictures buried bright
uncovered in dust and smiles
the beginning, the end

in wind prayed hands clasp
against a darken torment
clouding memories foggy
but always rehearsing

moment to moment autumn closes in

in shadows thought provokes; deals with the Devil
soul for soul as God's will undone
tears flow while the night refuses to remain faithful

another drink washes down more pain
releasing
tirades of justified speech
a dialect of proportion
slurred but reaching

"God gave his only son"
as the cross lies on the floor
ripped from the wall stained in blood
as the river of remorse flows

slowly a stumbling clock counts down
when life and death mix
the ever after of never after
even then the cold will remain
bringing back spring
and the 830 rain

lips sticky hold the end of a cigarette
as teetering becomes normalcy, tomorrow
never becomes the dream lost
and holding hold on seems like holding onto
nothing

time is a whisper in the breeze
haunting

illusionary

dirty black
hat crooked on
dirty blonde cut and fading
once hazel and green blurring
into brown the blue circles drawing
ever deeper deep into thoughts remorse
transpired in pupils dilated pure but
suffering a disease addict walking

dressed in toxic admission
scorn in jeans ripped by
the knee to ground pleading
callused words mending
pen to paper bleeding
slurred meanings tripping
in disguise a slow grind
while the Chucks
continue untied

illusionary tactics

from saving to wasted
a four leaf clover in the pocket
crumbling with the step by step
motion the slow burn
emotional overload
dear Lord down on knees soiled
hands arching

clouds roll silent before
thunder cast sonic tears
forming at the base
grave in the mistake that forever
was a state of confusion
a venom like no other
feigning the truth behind
a simple smile letting go

in midnight traumas shaking
earth to soul, soul to scream
without creating

the shadows fall in line
deserted dreams taking
piece by peace
in the rapid eye
fixed on the final

slow strangle

saturday Love

the polished cinder block wall,
with its pristine white grout,
held steady as a father
fell back collapsed knees bent

the stone facade of the floor,
shined a morning gleam,
as the father's head enveloped
into his hands, tears overflowing
the cracks between fingers

cold surrounded the room blue

the slow walk into, in two
hospital blankets pulled to the
chin, tape still holding the breathing
tube in, eyes closed, hand to hand
losing warmth, her hair was perfectly
perfect showing a father's eyebrows

passed down

as a baby, the father ran his
index finger over the crown of her nose
to help calm his stirring child
saturday Love, that action was repeated
to calm the soul peaceful
after the thirty minute struggle to regain,
to regain breath, hope, life, a daughter's sunrise

the glass door, with its room wide curtain,

couldn't contain forever heartbreak
in motion opening, as aunts, uncles,
grandmothers and grandfathers passed in and out,
the brothers' silent goodbye to his sister tore at the father's
heart, even as the baby boys sparkling blue eyes held
steady, the father's dirty brown started faltering

summer's blur, autumn's breeze shifting, winter's cold
embrace, a father's search for reasoning~

seven- 210 days of wide and sleepless dreams
terrorizing, need. the visitation weekly, the Garden
of Eternal, where the flowers have been removed, by
cold hands that never knew of the daughters love for Purple
on knees, a struggling brain and heart still make believe that
in the private conversations when the father speaks to his
daughter
that a reply is always just a moment away

just a moment away, waiting

dance

dance tempo
with a ballerinas hand she speaks
of beauty and peace
Jesus creating
utopia in dreams
cloud to heaven
passing
soul breaching
truth behind the smile
grinning
she speaks
as His crown of thorns
is scarring

glass

on the glass coffee table
with lightening striking
7 lines white call
while the Lord breaks into
whispering

dollar bill, dollar, dollar bill
rolled finger tight
gripped between the thumb and index
as the rain starts to fall
the Lord stands over
whispering

inhale…
nose to throat, throat to lungs
lungs to vessels, vessels to brain
releasing…

one down, six to remove

power drain
as the storm crashes overhead
flickering, the mind, a state, denial
leans back, chill, capturing the mood
in suicidal desperation line seven
withdraws into cavities transposed
as the Lord falls to his knees
pleading

crumbling
under the throw, the strands vine around the neck
3 in the morning choke
eyes closed
in the never after, vision fixed
in the never after, ash in breath
while in tongues, the Lord is chanting

echo, as the thunder slowly rolls away
the weakened body quivers
with the lasting memory
hand to arm cold flesh staining
dear Lord with his tarnished halo
broke, continues speaking, unknown

from the coast, the storm brews right to left
Indiana gales under coastal libations
in dictation, hand to pen, pen to pad
letter to words, daughter miss you love
as the lord starts last rights' praying

overdose

letter

fucking leech pulling on the skin
still bleeding slowing clotting
weakening a crippled heart breaking

with that poison breath loathing
sintastic hyperactive slope off the brain
taking your fucking words your throne

slit wrist pockets dreaming quarters and reunions
as your fucking voice continues clamoring
ceasing no end a bullet my friend closing

draino in the souls awakening since the cold
fucking took the heat the memory stories
twelve steps back the fuck away solidarity

ripping at open wounds tearing apart cleansing
dirty King of nothing with your fucking magic book
lying ripped apart just as you did to my daughter

a can of gasoline pristine and it speaks harboring
last wishes mother fucker said tight
as the dancing flame brings peace

April ninth

letter *remix*

fucking leech scraping bone to bone
gnawing ever deeper just another kill
weakening the broken heart six feet demeaning

with that poison fucking breath preaching
scripture in rapture sintastic murderous beginnings
take those words with your fucking throne

slit wrist pockets reaper man here are the quarters
payment for travel across the damned voices in the dark
ceasing no end a bullet to the brain

draino in the plunger setting deeper just to scar
allowing the union between two to overcome
earthly grasp soil covering back the fuck away solidarity

ripping at stitched up wounds tearing apart cleansing
dirty King of nothing with your useless condolences
lying ripped apart crucifix stabbed into the heart

a can of gasoline the battles begins and ends
a dancing flame set to regret revenge the taste of
last wishes mother fucking King before your world ends

April ninth

Charlie on the move

Oxy crushed in lines
listing by numbers every reason
1, two, 3
inhale

Charlie on the move, a fur ball
chasing ghost

and I have painted my body in red
the eyes are in black

one, 2, three
exhale.

Go, ready set
melting time into, in two, in
developing black and white pictures
from memories penned

Charlie on the move
and I let her dig her claws
ever deeper just to feel

and I have crossed out my veins
with a chaser of Drano and Mountain Dew

opened eyes spiraling blindness
but the purple phone
rings silent
as mother and father
have forgotten how to be
in the deafening absolution

Another line begging, shot gunned
with a Camel's bloody exhale pleading

Charlie on the move

while Blue tidal waves the darkness
the room falls dizzy

and I have dusted all the frames
that house my Dearest Daughter
gone but always

The first snow is approaching
as the wind starts its' shuffling
post traumatic suffering

Charlie on the move
running blindly into windows close

and I have sewn back these scars
trying to remain but the stars
fail to grasp the liquid nerves
spilled on the shag carpet

Charlie on the move

Accumulated Occupancy

the rise, sunset cold, full dark
foil covers muffle, the new born razor
if she can't speak then these tears
mute, shall become the dreams under
rivers of

frost in light, advice written
on windows, the fingerprints of past
shadows, lingering, telling no tales,
just murderous denial closing, as dirt
crosses hands dried, even as rains, drop
by drop suffocate

the eight by 3 plot surround
December leaves stick to granite and
marble, the bronze shines, with damp
warmth falling, saline toxicity, blurring
the vision, once visual, the vision now
straight lined, as rose, white, singular
stands, against the ever deepening winter

Windsor south

rolling clouds smoke
full moon pass
injection
whiskey in coke
ice melt slow

open bible
spoken tongues dementia
hollow gold
flowers binding
broken vase
fragmented

swallow

lighter flash
jets overhead
air stream turbulent
sound waves
carrying

reverberation
shaking window sliding
screen open
heart beat
cold air follow
breathe

Jesus on a swing
chain choking
liquid in the air
cigarette burning
down

commiseration
broken foot strangle
incapacitated whisper
distance
step by step
moving

nowhere

black and white

the Christmas lights hang down in strands
illumination
through the room

august peers nightly
a secret view peeping through the window
the curtains closed to dream

under the pillows hands fold pressurized
cracks in the ointment
silky smooth- touch

shuffling the cobwebs cling memory
entrapment
as the spiders eight legs tap eight am

temple scowl wrinkles from afar
wrong side
the mirror fogs as the last glimpse fades away

sun shine chronicles the day slowing
cigarette smolder
another inhale walking into in two

another pearl of indecent proposals
wearing down the slope of ever last
arms reaching white t-shirt stretching

cracks in concrete yellow lines stay in line
the white is outside boundaries
faded black chucks running

vicious

vicious tempo
with snake eyes he speaks
of life changing
Jesus taking
heart to beat
painfully
in mourning
devil's advocate
arguing
he speaks
as the soul continues
weeping

alkaline

through spine, stenosis
veins travel lightening
lantern dreams in clouds
thunder voices clap against
and she moves wind undone
flowing flower crow's feet
at the bed rail hanging

under cover silence
wings wail in broken fury
feathers air swirl
movement in shadows
the crow talons tight
scraping bronze out of snow
Saturday love
the betrayal

chemical demon toying
scratches on the back
opening a hole
fingered the wound
meant to check
the pounding heart
the blackness of lungs
in out in out motive
infected as another
line infested

ninety degree sanity
pulled chin high
with straps
clawing wrist and ankles
but she moves in and out
purple dress flowing flower
wilting in love dark
half eye blind
focused on the light at the end
dreaming as the garden
floods

faint in whisper
ears prickle at the memory
shunned to the back

but making its way forward
just as the wound began
leaking life
ounce by… she moves over
broken wings tangled
air swirls in turbulence
against dried tears stained
face to cheek, cheek to lips
lips to tongue tied
in wired hesitation
the monitor flat lined
a constant moan
as she regains her perch
talons shred the withered
leaves from the fall covering
bronze of Ashe
and quiet enters under
as eyelids flutter once
tomorrow never comes

alchemy

on a spring bobbing
Jesus
white robe enchant
crystal blue eye stare
hands air to sky

but her blood is on the linoleum
clotting before mechanical bend
forced removal
but there is shaking in membrane
thought production scissor
as the doctors rush
but the machines have
became silent in tone
whisper mourn

after clouds moved
in the peak
midafternoon
blonde hair stain
liquid in breath
fluid without words

in blame

laying down

whiskey on rocks
a cigarette clench
ashes wisp the breeze
falling
knees to ground soul to…
tourniquet high
the picture fades

reunion

rotation

in sheets melting, gravitating
to the cold whisper of
eyes rapid movement,

isolation

primal scream, a heart on the sleeve
pounding, bleeding, seizing
time, machine head, counting
till the seconds stop and the
dark takes away all the stars but one
around the neck
the future chained to the past

liquid red streams along the corrugated
picture frames sitting motionless
the smile fades into blurry images
taken to capture the soul breaking
in two, the roses have dried and crumble
onto feet planted deep in the soil
of never letting go

the feeling stays true
as memories refocus on a newborn's weight
warm and soothing
to the weight of the cold box
held in shaky hands
as they place the child
into the ground

a quiet stirring rustles the sheets
as the air rushes over
and the leaking roof spills
the skies own tears burning across the cheek
forcing the pictures to freeze and strain
mental confusion just as the alarm rings

snow is covering Saturn
as winter tries for a third time to
bring the cold back to life
going under

as the eyes will be closed again
fostering the belief that sooner rather than later
laughter and love
daughter and father
heart and soul
a reunion will take place

in another life

life

unsettling-
a smooth hinge opening
the door
to fresh roses drying in
slow motion
their silky white petals
turning brown falling
covering the frost
from the burial

it's so cold
in distance
time is
standing
still, the Doctors
remove all the layers
attempting
to restart a heart
beating
that has closed
ventricles and valves
to those that have witnessed
the shattering
effect of losing
a daughter's touch

it is January love in winter's castle
plush in razor scarred arms
with needle tracks evaporating
flame driven liquid hemorrhage

with silence forming
in mourning, I bend
and pray to the one thing
I could never believe in
in the hopes that you
could be here again
so I could say
all the things
that a father should tell
his daughter
so I could
walk you down that aisle

and give you away
with a full heart and a smile
so I could

another inhale as I walk into
the morning looking
to the stars
for a sign
for a reason
but the exhale forces
the escape
and creates another moment
when reality becomes the nightmare
constant
and I lower my head as tears form

it is the eyes
that always give me away

reaper man

iron gates holding
a swell of breath escape
temptation breaking smooth

black in two
mainlined truth in
rural vein revolutions

painted in red
justice poetic
bloody lip piercing silence

the baby cries

a cigarette smolder
under weighted ash
charcoal dreams run

in motion
wind bringing change
storm clouds production

a new scar open
drown in killings
liquid lies blended

the baby cries

human suffering
the toll paying
quarters face up

crumble soul to
the last ounce
believe in

last of the cigarette
pressing against lips
as the enemy returns

Jesus on a chain

crimson

crimson tempo
fist through the grave he speaks
of never ending
Jesus and His fucking halo
tarnishing
eye to eyes
future skies
crumbling
storm clouds
pouring
he speaks
with the weight of loss
punishing

heartbeat

it was late fall 1992 when I met you
a piece of heaven with sparkling eyes
a wish, the dream, a little bit of God
held softly in my hands
I could feel your soul's weight with each
beat of your tiny heart
as this father held you, dear daughter,
for the first time

heartbeat
struggle in winter 12 as nine months pass
without a night full of memories
flashing in and out of dreams,
my little girl all grown, a beautiful woman,
as shades of purple and red
hazel color this world through tear soaked eyes

heartbeat
it was us against the world that seemed to be opening
a rain cloud with bright skies on the horizon
a chemical bond well beyond shared beginnings
and I have stopped my deadliest habit even as these scars
plead, but the emotional damage is reeling
causing these lungs to fill only half full
as breathing without is being without

heartbeat
and April still lingers
my little girl now all alone in a cold room
the machines silent
and when that call came 830 rain
nothing could slow Saturn from you
but late is and my back felt the cold wall
as I collapsed from the words that your mother
spoke and walking into that blue room
breathing tube still
and as I sat down next to you
hand in hand I tried
to feel your heartbeat
once again

heartbeat
somewhere in the back of my mind

the hope that you will still come home lingers
Doctor Doctor says it is all a part of grieving
part of the healing, but I stopped listening
and Blue is upon a shelf, emotional state of emergency
as I miss talking about nothing and everything
I miss the IMA and star gazing
code red and random road trips
I miss you my little girl

heartbeat
and I promise I will go on as long as I can
"I will see you again" and these words are
just as much yours as mine, but soon this
pen may fall silent while I feverishly scribe
on my skin stars and dreams, a heartbeat,
your heartbeat,
everlasting

paper eyes

scribbled brown taint
outside the lines

ribbons tied rings

pixels form ice
prisms of rainbows

springtime fantasies
focusing

mid-January flaunt

snow flurries carry
voices blend

taped mouth grit
moaning

double vision

pupils flex
unwinding

invisible ending
pretending

eyes remain
closed

day dreaming

2 into 1

2 into 1 tempo
with a lashing tongue he speaks
of battling
the unrighteous
Jesus off that throne
step for step
throwing stones
forsaken
the precious daughter
missing
he speaks
equality in blame
poisoning

tonic

the drop
doctor says doctor says
as the last of the injection
is forced into the tube
500 cc's of happiness
a slow burn in the arm
tingling to cold membranes
numb

as the plunger hits bottom
brain seize teeth clench
around the leather straps
holding ankles and wrist bound
but doctor says doctor says
let the tonic potion fill the fever
with anti-climactic hypnotic visions
hallucinating

so much dreaming
dreaming of laughter
laughing through a closed door
eyes blind
binding in the ward
in the world becoming
teeth clench brain seize
doctor says doctor says
relax

fluorescents shine
as the four wheeled cart vibrates
through man made colors
black and white screaming
doctor says doctor says
that the wrist and ankles will be freed
when the tonic starts its healing
forcing away the make believe
that she is still
breathing

10 month debilitation
full of rehabilitation
doctor says doctor says
as the release initiates

signed documentation
that well is a disease
hinging on a digression
of depressing
reality

conjoined

the morning after psychosis
vision in fraudulent ghost and wind
palpable fragrance in scheme
alone

clean body fragile mind
paranoid hurt refusing to scrub
blessed in red under
stain, the water remains, scorching

the hold last forever
with eyes closed

      tremors
haunt memories closing in
as frost predicates
slowing heart… beat

July passes onto march

the strands of day run
into the black night
while shards of light
reflect bows of promised
momentum

breathing in the foul air
a whore to the dream
lips mouth yesterday's smile
a continuation of the slave

with silence an exhale
torn skin rising
as the name falls
draining

for ced cohesion

rainy Saturday with wind soaking broken wings,
follow
in the morning after, in the morning shadow, laying,
hollow
and upon the rising she said love, as the, the final drop
left her lips, tomorrow

glued submission, movement, move moment, move, slow
into the never after, when once, once there was, once
she was, as time returned, re

count down, ten nine eight seven… breathe, breath, escape
sober
step by step left foot right ink forced in two scar
closer
and the heart lies, constant, stationary, solitary

sanity-

hand to chest, chest to thought, thought to feel
she said if, I said would

jumping

sibling

the boy
with his piercing blue
eyes never blinking
once in a while focuses

before the scars
melting
titanium and screws
holding his thoughts

when time was

he is becoming
such a little man
since you have been
gone

and sometimes in
the rarest of moments
his lips break their
silence and remembers

since you have been
he has spoken of
your laugh that filled
rooms now distant

music that the house
used to glow
and your voice
singing in the quiet

when time was

the boy with his brightly blue
posted on the fridge
"Jump Rope"
his favorite song because of you

but he will never
know the true relationship
that was taken
before it could grow

and sometimes when he
goes quiet
i can see that sadness
of a brother missing his sister

when time was

fracture

in the cool morning
May flowers brown from the lack of water
on the deck fresh wood stained
the same brown, decay

the first cigarette smolders
in slightly chapped lips

inhale

a stretch of skin
hands raised skyward
not in praise but in function
following form

and they took

last night's ritual
of spreading wings to fly
strangled in sheets
with shadowed hands pulling tighter

the ring of sweat
still lingering around the neck
even as the mirror
pokes fun of sunken eyes

steam clean
remorse and regret
as the shower runs hot
107 degrees

careful to mind the scar
while scrubbing the soul
a torn apart soul
still broken

and with hands on tile
leveraging
the balancing act
steading what has become unsteady

they took

as the towel dries clean
shuttering
wide eyes with their circles
black, stare into nothing

one step closer
as the days run further
between when
hands held hands cold

with a flip of the thumb
a new Marlboro flames to life

exhale

this retreat has become
a prison with headaches
forcing blinds
to shut out

and comfortable has
remained
uncomfortable in
the past reminders

they took

wearing purple
always
in religion
bled into skin

as time has moved
leaving behind
all but the memory
all but the heart

in disguise
personal hijack
13 months of darkness
streaming down the cheek

mid-day wane
a stumble in shaking hands
running fingers over
colored pixels fading

they took

disbelief grows
in the two year cycle
of circular grief
as depression takes hold

twenty cigarettes a day
fail to meet the alleviated
need to withdraw
further into one

it is a crusade
to quicken the pace
when 6 feet will finally rest
and this father can be with his daughter

they took

thumb drives full of personal suicide
typed in black and white life

line by line breath by breath
marching into the dark falling
in

the silhouette of shadow puppets
on the wall sinking their grip deeper

struggling to find the right space
in a space alone, closed

step by step the daily routine
of making it to the next

even as tomorrow has
withheld its promise

a failure to understand
loss of, the beating heart races

all roads lead to
the end, the beginning

they took

in April, found in grey colored walls
stability defied gravity
defined
as hands held back collapsing in
the beckoning disillusion of peace
in dreams counting backwards
time, steps, days
the fracture of continual
repeating

concentrated belief
forced out of sight and into
she is constantly
breathing
without the tube
removed

mother tries to hold me calm
as visit upon visit
to the graveyard
sets motion in overload
emotive

they took

my mind races
back
to the simple procedure
without
consequences
without

my mind races back
to your mother on the phone
desperate for me to
get to the hospital

my mind races back
to the morning the doctors
took the very best part of me
away

Caroline

but her chucks sit by the door
waiting for when she comes

and my friends tell me
that the stars
brightly should hold
comfort when

and I never understood just how much
and I should have told her more
but my tongue for years never
and regret sinks in
as these tears lend their own

fold

listening to a speaking God on TV
3 in the morning insomnia heartbreaking
and knowing that prayers are the answers
never begging but I remember
just how much and I can still feel
the cold skin on skin trying to mend
these hands left clasped
wondering when
and sometimes I try to carry a conversation
but my tongue becomes
and words only form
my friends know but I could never

living in black and white
letting closeness come only
with distance time stops and I
burn my lungs trying to
scream at the top but mirrors
stare back in disagreement
as it has become so dark in
light I can still see your smile

the laugh that laugh laughing at everything
nothing still fills this heart trying
the beating is self-inflicted
I take pictures mental of the last time

when, then, seems like yesterday but
so far away as another day passes
and the night so cruel plays games
lights moving visions of superficial but
I believe that you have
but it is nonsense grasping for
peace

pale

changing recognition everyday something
everything reminds and finding
your face in people I would never
but the reminders follow like a candle
flowing wax over the floor I
fall down on these knees
trying to form a connection
in dirt and grass my hands wipe away
the fallen leaves and out of place grass clippings
keeping stone and bronze clean

circular disjointed belief in
the process of grief healing
even as saline brings life out of focus
and the streaks of hurt show on
I stumble through
knowing the unknown

but her chucks sit by the door
waiting for when she comes
home

Untitled

Held, your hand, so close, so close to, you were the rock, the light glimmering, the one star burning bright. And as the room turns, and as the world continues its dizzy spin, and as I have lost my balance, I still look to you for strength. Even as I, forget my way, forget words and verse, strip my soul naked with tears, I still hold your hand for peace, even though 16 months have passed and your touch has grown silence, I can still feel your heart beating, leading me to find the beauty in the closed off places where my mind wanders. And when the time comes, I know you will lead me home. Holding my hand like I did yours.

www.ingramcontent.com/pod-product-compliance
Lightning Source LLC
Chambersburg PA
CBHW031414040426
42444CB00005B/567